Summer Time Carols

AuthorHouse™
1663 Liberty Drive
Bloomington, IN 47403
www.authorhouse.com
Phone: 1-800-839-8640

© 2009 Lindsay Rindt. All rights reserved.

No part of this book may be reproduced, stored in a retrieval system, or transmitted by any means without the written permission of the author.

First published by AuthorHouse 12/31/2009

ISBN: 978-1-4490-5774-9 (sc)

Printed in the United States of America
Bloomington, Indiana

This book is printed on acid-free paper.

This Book Belongs To: _____

Without your encouragement, these pages would be blank.
                                              -Lindsay

For my wife, Crystal.
                    -Chris

Summer Time Carols

written by Lindsay Rindt

illustrated by Christopher Provencher

Based on a true childhood.

Gloria loved each season. She adored how the leaves changed color in autumn and awed at the beautiful snowfall of winter. She celebrated spring with the arrival of blooming tulips, daffodils and the smell of freshly cut grass.

But every summer, in the midst of all the fun, Gloria couldn't help but wish it was December. There was something special about winter, which no other season had: Christmas Carols. Gloria loved Christmas Carols.

One night while Gloria's Papa was tucking her in for bed she confided, "I wish it were winter. I want to listen to Christmas Carols."

Her Papa replied, "Who says you can't listen to Christmas carols whenever you want?" Gloria felt relief - what a simple solution her Papa had provided!

However, later that night, Gloria found she could not sleep. She was so excited to listen to her carols CD, morning wouldn't come fast enough. So, she found her discman and listened to every song.

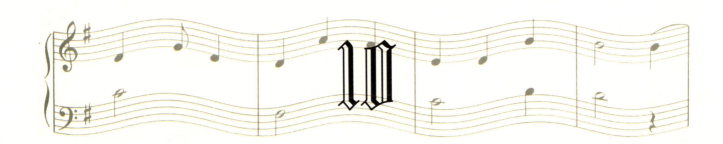

Once Gloria heard the first of her favorite songs, she couldn't help but listen to them every chance she got. It seemed that everywhere Gloria went, Christmas music surely followed. Of course, not everyone shared in her excitement, but that didn't really matter to Gloria. She could not get enough Christmas carols.

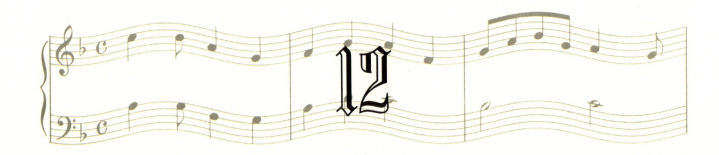

As autumn arrived Gloria's passion for carols did not let up. She hummed them on the way to school and whistled them as family gathered for Thanksgiving dinner. Although, she did rest just a short while during the carving of the turkey and the serving of her Nanna's famous pumpkin pie.

By the time it was Halloween, she was really in the spirit of things. Gloria and her Mama spent hours perfecting her Halloween costume. While Allan was a turtle and Scotty was a mouse, Gloria of course, was a caroler. She was extra sure to sing a special song for each house visited.

17

Before Gloria knew it the first snowflakes of winter had arrived. After a day of sledding and hot chocolate, Gloria listen silently to her music as she watched the snow fall outside her bedroom window.

It was the night of Barrowtown Elementary's Christmas Recital, Gloria could hardly wait to sing all of her favorite songs. But as the choir began, she found herself unable to sing a single word. Not that Gloria was tired of them, she just wanted to listen to everyone else finally embrace the magic of the music. And as the choir sang, the spirit of Christmas filled the air.

The singing of carols always flooded Gloria's mind with the happy memories of Christmas. They meant the gathering of friends and family and as Gloria sat by the fire, she realized that the carols had brought her to this day. Content, she put her music away until next year.

Spring soon passed and summer arrived once more. One day, when Gloria was cleaning her room, she found her old carols CD; it had not been played in many months. She dusted off the cover and popped the disc into her player...

24

As Gloria listened, she began to hum, then whistle, before bursting into song! And as it had before, the music brought her to a place a hope and excitement.

27

It wasn't long before she was decking the halls once again. And while her brothers were outside swimming and roasting marshmallows, Gloria enjoyed the soundtrack to her life, Summer Time Carols.

And then it snowed...

About the Author

Lindsay Rindt loves Christmas Carols. She is lovingly supported by her husband Rob and son Oliver (who have been decking the halls since July). Lindsay lives nestled amongst the farmlands of the Fraser Valley.

About the Illustrator

Christopher Provencher is a cartoonist, graphic designer, illustrator and even, surprisingly enough, a husband. He also lives in the Fraser Valley, with his wife, Crystal and their scruffy, little dog, Harley.

photo courtesy of Pixstar Photobooth

LaVergne, TN USA
27 January 2010
171276LV00004BA